CAT CRAZY

by Anthony

Published in the UK by
POWERFRESH Limited
3 Gray Street
Northampton
England
NN1 3QQ

Telephone 01604 30996
Facsimile 01604 21013

Cover and interior layout Powerfresh

CAT CRAZY
ISBN 1 874125 481

Printed in the UK by Avalon Print Ltd., Northampton.
        Powerfresh January 1996

TITLES BY POWERFRESH
· NORTHAMPTON · ENGLAND ·

Please Send Me:

CRINKLED 'N' WRINKLED	£2.99	☐	WE'RE GETTING MARRIED	£2.99	☐
DRIVEN CRAZY	£2.99	☐	MONSTORS	£2.99	☐
OH NO IT'S XMAS AGAIN	£2.99	☐	THE ART OF SLOBOLOGY	£2.99	☐
TRUE LOVE	£2.99	☐	THE DEFINATIVE GUIDE TO VASECTOMY	£2.99	☐
IT'S A BOY	£2.99	☐	KEEP FIT WITH YOUR CAT	£2.99	☐
IT'S A GIRL	£2.99	☐	MARITAL BLISS AND OTHER OXYMORONS	£2.99	☐
NOW WE ARE 40	£2.99	☐	THE OFFICE FROM HELL	£2.99	☐
FUNNY SIDE OF 40 HIM	£2.99	☐	PMT CRAZED	£2.99	☐
FUNNY SIDE OF 40 HER	£2.99	☐	SEXY CROTCHWORD PUZZLES	£2.99	☐
FUNNY SIDE OF 50 HIM	£2.99	☐	STONED AGE MAN	£2.99	☐
FUNNY SIDE OF 50 HER	£2.99	☐	OUT TO LUNCH	£2.99	☐
FUNNY SIDE OF 60'S	£2.99	☐	HORNY MAN'S ADULT DOODLE BOOK	£2.99	☐
FUNNY SIDE OF SEX	£2.99	☐	HORNY GIRL'S ADULT DOODLE BOOK	£2.99	☐
THE COMPLETE BASTARDS GUIDE TO GOLF	£2.99	☐	IF BABIES COULD TALK	£2.99	☐
IT'S NO FUN BEING A MOTHER	£2.99	☐	CAT CRAZY	£2.99	☐

I have enclosed cheque / postal order for £......... made payable to **GUNNERS**

NAME...ADDRESS ....

....

COUNTY...POSTCODE ....

Please return to: **Powerfresh Ltd. 3 Gray Street, Northampton, NN1 3QQ, ENGLAND.**
EEC countries add £1 Postage, Packaging & Order processing. Outside EEC please add £3.00